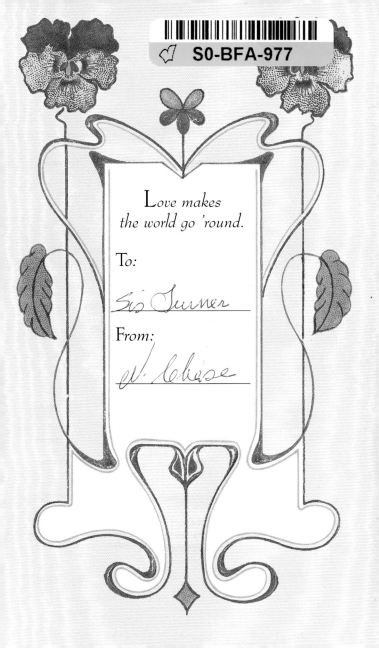

S0-BFA-977

Love makes
the world go 'round.

To:

Sis Turner

From:

N. Chase

Also by Barbara Milo Ohrbach

The Scented Room
The Scented Room Gardening Notebook
Antiques at Home
Simply Flowers
A Token of Friendship
Memories of Childhood
A Bouquet of Flowers
A Cheerful Heart
The Spirit of America
Merry Christmas
Happy Birthday
All Things Are Possible
Food for the Soul
Tabletops
If You Think You Can
Roses for the Scented Room

BARBARA MILO OHRBACH

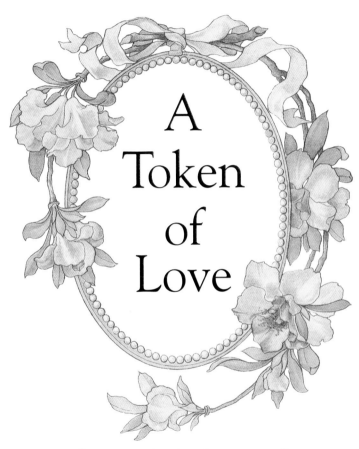

A Token of Love

A little book of romance

CLARKSON POTTER/PUBLISHERS

Published by Clarkson Potter/Publishers
New York, New York.
Member of the Crown Publishing Group.

Random House, Inc. New York, Toronto,
London, Sydney, Auckland
www.randomhouse.com

CLARKSON N. POTTER
is a trademark and POTTER
and colophon are registered trademarks
of Random House, Inc.

Printed in Singapore

DESIGN BY LISA SLOANE

Library of Congress Cataloging-in-Publication Data
A token of love: [compiled by] Barbara Milo Ohrbach.
1. Love–Quotations, maxims, etc. I. Ohrbach, Barbara Milo
PN6084.L6 T64 2001
302.3–dc21   99-089064
ISBN 0-609-60501-1
10 9 8 7 6 5 4 3 2 1
First Edition

A *happy marriage is a long conversation that seems all too short.*

ANDRÉ MAUROIS

Looking back on my own thirty years of marriage, I realize how accurate those words really are. My experience is far from unique, for there are countless couples who will say the same: when you find your soulmate, the "conversation" between you—that is, the mutual exchange of ideas and endearments, of hopes and plans, the sharing of disappointments and triumphs—evolves effortlessly, as if you were communing with another part of yourself.

Human beings are love-seeking creatures by nature, and the desire to experience life's adventure with a cherished "other" seems to be an essential part of our make-up.

Loftier minds than mine have written about the sanctity of marriage and its obligations, which is all very fine, if a bit daunting. And while I agree with the old saying that "a trouble shared is a trouble halved," the converse—"a pleasure shared is a pleasure doubled"—is equally true. Or, as Dorothy L. Sayers' fictional detective Lord Peter Wimsey explained to his beloved Harriet Vane, other considerations aside, he'd marry her "just for the fun of the thing." I sometimes think that "the fun of the thing"— the shared laughter, the simple delight in each other's company—is one of the greatest satisfactions in married life.

With these thoughts in mind, then, this little collection of observations about love, marriage, and, yes, romance, is dedicated to soulmates everywhere—whether newly met or soon-to-be wed. I offer it in tribute, also, to those long-married couples, whose love has grown and ripened with time.

Lord Peter finally married his Harriet and when she expresses her love for him, his response describes the secret which every lover knows at heart:

And what do all the great words come to in the end, but that?—I love you—I am at rest with you—I have come home.

BARBARA MILO OHRBACH

There is no surprise more magical
than the surprise of being loved:
It is God's finger on man's shoulder.

CHARLES MORGAN

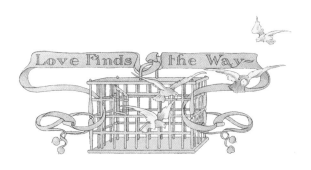

Happiness seems made to be shared.

JEAN RACINE

A happy marriage has in it
all the pleasures of friendship,
all the enjoyments of sense and reason,
and indeed, all the sweets of life.

JOSEPH ADDISON

To love

and be loved is

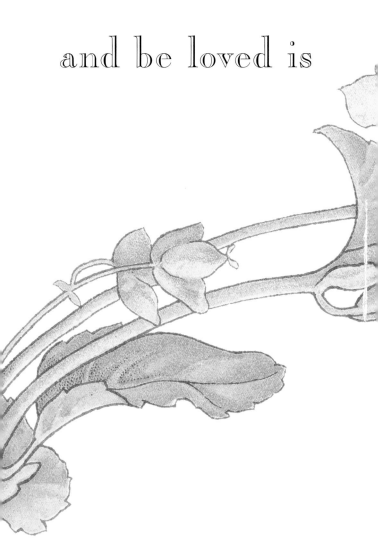

to feel the sun

from both sides.

DAVID VISCOTT

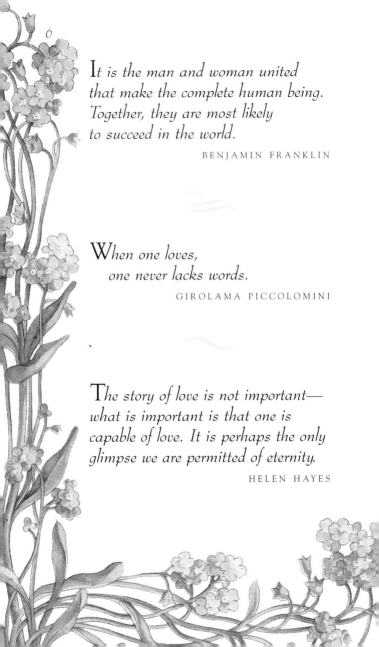

It is the man and woman united
that make the complete human being.
Together, they are most likely
to succeed in the world.

BENJAMIN FRANKLIN

When one loves,
one never lacks words.

GIROLAMA PICCOLOMINI

The story of love is not important—
what is important is that one is
capable of love. It is perhaps the only
glimpse we are permitted of eternity.

HELEN HAYES

Love works miracles every day:
such as weakening the strong,
and strengthening the weak;
making fools of the wise,
and wise men of fools;
favoring the passions,
destroying reason, and, in a word,
turning everything topsy-turvy.

MARGUERITE DE VALOIS

To see a young couple loving each
     other is no wonder;
but to see an old couple loving each
     other is the best sight of all.

WILLIAM MAKEPEACE THACKERAY

Love is an energy which exists
of itself. It is its own value.

THORNTON WILDER

Love is the poetry

of the senses.

HONORÉ DE BALZAC

Love is a fruit in season at all times,
and within reach of every hand.

MOTHER TERESA

There is time for work,
and time for love.
That leaves no other time.

COCO CHANEL

A successful marriage requires
falling in love many times,
with the same person.

MIGNON McLAUGHLIN

Love and a cough cannot be hid.

GEORGE HERBERT

Since we parted yester eve,
I do love thee, love believe,
Twelve times dearer,
    twelve hours longer—
One dream deeper,
    one night stronger,
One sun surer—
    thus much more
Than I loved thee,
    love, before.

SIR EDWARD
BULWER-LYTTON

I LOVE

Je t'aime *French*

Ich liebe Dich *German*

Ya lyooblyoo tibyah *Russian*

Aku cinta padamu *Bahasa Indonesian*

Ti amo *Italian*

Te quiero *Spanish*

You

Ik hou van jou   *Dutch*

Jag älskar dig   *Swedish*

Ja cie kocham   *Polish*

Seni seviyorum   *Turkish*

Kimi o ai shiteru   *Japanese*

Eu te amo   *Portuguese*

I *love you more than yesterday,*
less than tomorrow.

EDMOND ROSTAND

T*o love someone means to see him*
as God intended him.

FYODOR DOSTOYEVSKY

O*ne word frees us of all the weight*
and pain of life; that word is love.

SOPHOCLES

A*ll mankind loves a lover.*

RALPH WALDO EMERSON

The supreme happiness of life is
the conviction that we are loved.

VICTOR HUGO

There is nothing nobler or
more admirable than when
two people who see eye to eye
keep house as man and wife,
confounding their enemies
and delighting their friends.

HOMER

A man should select for his wife
only such a woman as he would
select for a friend, were she a man.

JOSEPH JOUBERT

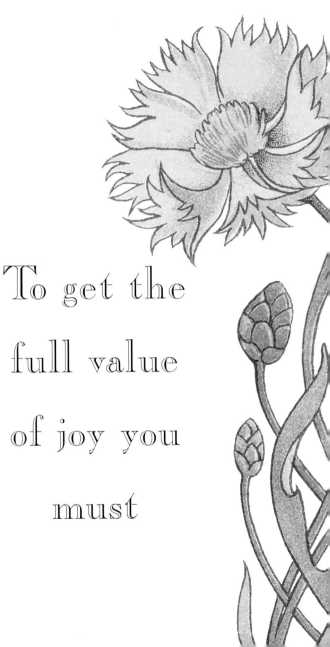

To get the
full value
of joy you
must

have

somebody

to divide it

with.

MARK TWAIN

Personally, the only four-letter word
I would use is LOVE.

MAE WEST

All happiness depends
on a leisurely breakfast.

JOHN GUNTHER

The critical period in matrimony
is breakfast time.

SIR ALAN PATRICK HERBERT

Personally I know nothing about sex
because I've always been married.

ZSA ZSA GABOR

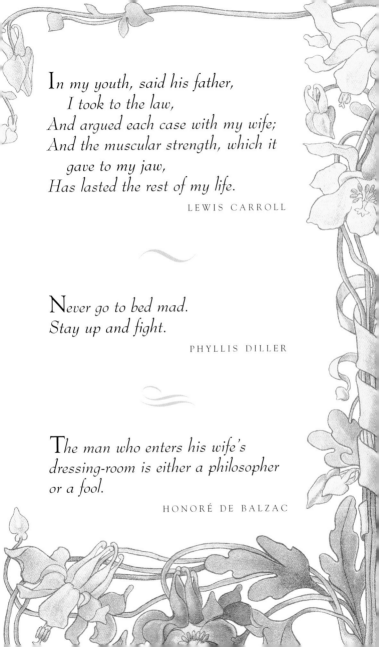

In my youth, said his father,
    I took to the law,
And argued each case with my wife;
And the muscular strength, which it
    gave to my jaw,
Has lasted the rest of my life.

LEWIS CARROLL

Never go to bed mad.
Stay up and fight.

PHYLLIS DILLER

The man who enters his wife's
dressing-room is either a philosopher
or a fool.

HONORÉ DE BALZAC

If you
  judge people,
you have
    no time
    to love them.

MOTHER TERESA

I seem to have loved you in numberless
forms, numberless times, in life after life,
in age after age forever.

RABINDRANATH TAGORE

Give me my Romeo;
　and when he shall die,
Take him and cut him out
　in little stars,
And he will make the face
　of heaven so fine
That all the world will be
　in love with night
And pay no worship
　to the garish sun.

WILLIAM SHAKESPEARE

And I will make thee a bed of roses,
and a thousand fragrant posies.

CHRISTOPHER MARLOWE

The good, the bad, hardship,
the joy, the tragedy, love
and happiness are all interwoven
into an indescribable whole
that is called life.

JACQUELINE KENNEDY ONASSIS

You must not kiss and tell.

WILLIAM CONGREVE

Sentiments

With all one's heart

Touch the heart

Win someone's heart

Heart to heart

From the bottom of my heart

Bless your heart

A heart of gold

Softhearted

OF THE HEART

Wholeheartedly

Heartfelt

Have a heart

Give one's heart

*Wear one's heart
on one's sleeve*

With heart and hand

Sweetheart

In our life there is a single color,
as on an artist's palette,
which provides the meaning of life
and art. It is the color of love.

MARC CHAGALL

Come live with me, and be my Love;
and we will all the pleasures prove.

CHRISTOPHER MARLOWE

Love cannot be forced,
love cannot be coaxed and teased.
It comes out of Heaven,
unasked and unsought.

PEARL S. BUCK

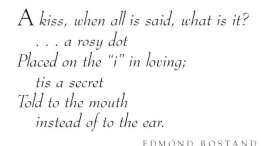

A kiss, when all is said, what is it?
  . . . a rosy dot
Placed on the "i" in loving;
  tis a secret
Told to the mouth
  instead of to the ear.

EDMOND ROSTAND

I can express no kinder sign of love,
Than this kind kiss.

WILLIAM SHAKESPEARE

Something made of nothing,
  tasting very sweet,
A most delicious compound,
  with ingredients complete.

MARY E. BUELL

Rule
for happiness:
something to do,
someone to love,
something
to hope for.

IMMANUEL KANT

Earth laughs in flowers.

RALPH WALDO EMERSON

Life is a flower of which love
is the honey.

VICTOR HUGO

Those who love deeply
never grow old.

SIR ARTHUR WING PINERO

Marriage is the proper remedy.

BENJAMIN FRANKLIN

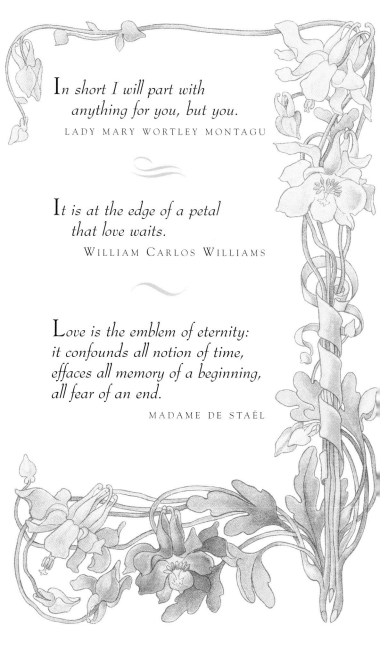

In short I will part with
anything for you, but you.

LADY MARY WORTLEY MONTAGU

It is at the edge of a petal
that love waits.

WILLIAM CARLOS WILLIAMS

Love is the emblem of eternity:
it confounds all notion of time,
effaces all memory of a beginning,
all fear of an end.

MADAME DE STAËL

Of all earthly music,

that which reaches

farthest

into heaven

is the beating of

a truly loving heart.

HENRY WARD BEECHER

A man without a wife is like
a vase without flowers.

AFRICAN PROVERB

To have and to hold
from this day forward,
for better, for worse,
for richer, for poorer,
in sickness, and in health,
to love and to cherish,
till death us do part.

BOOK OF COMMON PRAYER

If your wife is short,
bend down and listen to her.

THE TALMUD

A good marriage is that
in which each appoints the other
guardian of his solitude.

RAINER MARIA RILKE

The most precious possession
that ever comes to a man in this world
is a woman's heart.

J. G. HOLLAND

The Eskimos had 52 names for snow
because it was important to them: there
ought to be as many for love.

MARGARET ATWOOD

If you wish to be loved, love.

SENECA

CONGRAT

Blahoprani! *Czech*

Gefeliciteerd! *Dutch*

Félicitations! *French*

Comhghairdeas! *Gaelic*

Glückwünsche! *German*

Mazel tov! *Hebrew*

ULATIONS

Gratulàlok!	*Hungarian*
Congratulazioni!	*Italian*
Omedeto!	*Japanese*
¡Felicitaciones!	*Spanish*
Grattis!	*Swedish*
Čestitam!	*Serbo Croatian*

The best friend is likely to acquire
the best wife, because a good
marriage is based on the talent
for friendship.

FRIEDRICH NIETZSCHE

At the touch of love
everyone becomes a poet.

PLATO

Love is a great beautifier.

LOUISA MAY ALCOTT

The heart can do anything.

MOLIÈRE

Whatever our souls are made of,
his and mine are the same.

EMILY BRONTË

Love is a canvas furnished by
Nature, and embroidered
by imagination.

VOLTAIRE

Let your life lightly dance
on the edges of Time like
dew on the tip of a leaf.

RABINDRANATH TAGORE

Love conquers all.

VIRGIL

Love has nothing
to do with what
you are expecting to
get—only with what
you are expecting
to give—which is
everything.

KATHARINE HEPBURN

Those who bring sunshine
to the lives of others
cannot keep it from themselves.

SIR JAMES BARRIE

I like not only to be loved,
    but to be told I am loved.

GEORGE ELIOT

There is only one situation
I can think of in which men
and women make an effort
to read better than they usually do:
when they are in love
and reading a love letter.

MORTIMER ADLER

How do I love thee?
Let me count the ways.

ELIZABETH BARRETT BROWNING

Whither thou goest, I will go;
and where thou lodgest, I will lodge;
thy people shall be my people,
and thy God my God.

RUTH 1:16

Life is made up, not of great
sacrifices or duties, but of little things,
in which smiles and kindness,
and small obligations given habitually,
are what preserve the heart
and secure comfort.

HUMPHREY DAVY

There is only one

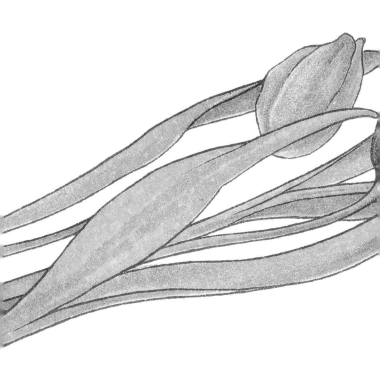

happiness in life,

to love

and be loved.

There is no sight on earth
more appealing than the sight
of a woman making dinner
for someone she loves.

THOMAS WOLFE

The way to a man's heart
is through his stomach.

MRS. SARAH PAYSON PARTON

The torch of love is lit
in the kitchen.

FRENCH PROVERB

Kissing don't last: cookery do.

GEORGE MEREDITH

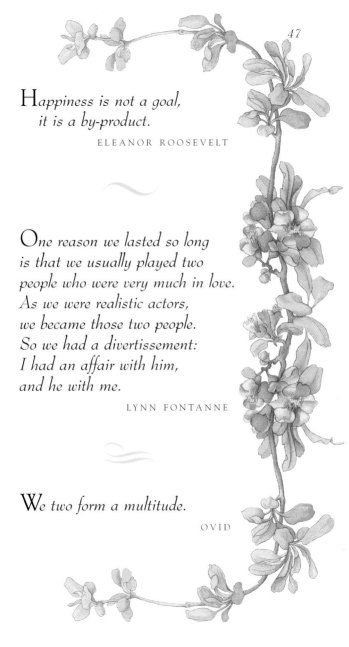

Happiness is not a goal,
 it is a by-product.

ELEANOR ROOSEVELT

One reason we lasted so long
is that we usually played two
people who were very much in love.
As we were realistic actors,
we became those two people.
So we had a divertissement:
I had an affair with him,
and he with me.

LYNN FONTANNE

We two form a multitude.

OVID

ANNIVER

1 **paper**

2 cotton

3 leather

4 books

5 wood

6 iron

7 **copper**

8 electrical
   appliances

9 pottery

10 tin

SARY GIFTS

11	steel
12	linen
13	lace
14	ivory
15	**crystal**
20	china
25	silver
30	pearl
35	jade
40	ruby
45	sapphire
50	gold

Love keeps the cold out better than a cloak.

HENRY WADSWORTH LONGFELLOW

Blest is the bride on whom
the sun doth shine.

ROBERT HERRICK

Destiny is not
a matter of chance,
it is a matter of choice;
it is not a thing to be waited for,
it is a thing to be achieved.

WILLIAM JENNINGS BRYAN

Love is love's reward.

JOHN DRYDEN

Drink to me only with thine eyes,
and I will pledge with mine;
or leave a kiss but in the cup
and I'll not look for wine.

BEN JONSON

Love is, above all, the gift of oneself.

JEAN ANOUILH

For years my wedding ring has
done its job. It has led me not into
temptation. It has reminded my
husband numerous times at parties
that it's time to go home. It has
been a source of relief to a dinner
companion. It has been a status
symbol in the maternity ward.

ERMA BOMBECK

Grow old
along with me!
The best
is yet to be.

ROBERT BROWNING

To make a marriage happy
You need a lot of love
And, added to it, thoughtfulness,
The things you're dreaming of:
Patience, understanding,
Good times and laughter, too,
Mixed in with pride and caring
And sharing all you do.

ANONYMOUS

Thoughts for Companions

An ear that waits to catch
A hand upon the latch;
A step that hastens its sweet rest to win;
A world of care without,
A world of strife shut out,
A world of love shut in.

DORA GREENWELL